W9-AGP-169

Bungee Jumping

by Jason Glaser

Consultant:
Casey A. Dale, President
North American Bungee Association (NABA)
Bungee Safety Consultants

CAPSTONE
HIGH/LOW BOOKS
an imprint of Capstone Press
Mankato, Minnesota

Capstone High/Low Books are published by Capstone Press
818 North Willow Street, Mankato, Minnesota 56001
http://www.capstone-press.com

Printed in the United States of America.

Library of Congress Cataloging-in-Publication Data
Glaser, Jason.
Bungee jumping/by Jason Glaser.
p. cm.—(Extreme sports)
Includes bibliographical references (p. 45) and index.
Summary: Discusses the history, stunts, competitions, equipment, and safety measures of bungee jumping.
ISBN 0-7368-0168-5
1. Bungee jumping—Juvenile literature. [1. Bungee jumping.] I. Title. II. Series.
GV770.27.G53 1999
797.5—dc21
98-45516
CIP
AC

Editorial Credits

Matt Doeden, editor; Timothy Halldin, cover designer; Sheri Gosewisch and Kimberly Danger, photo researchers

Photo Credits

Images International/Erwin C. "Bud" Nielson, 36, 38
Index Stock Imagery, 34–35
International Stock/Eric Sanford, cover, 32; Steve Lucas & Greg Johnston, 23; Mark Newman, 42
Jay Ireland & Georgienne Bradley, 4, 8, 12, 28, 41
Patrick Batchelder, 25
Photo Network, 17, 26, 31
Photophile/Mark E. Gibson, 7
Unicorn Stock Photos/Jean Higgins, 11, 18; David Cummings, 20

Table of Contents

Chapter 1
Bungee Jumping

Bungee jumping is a sport in which people jump from high places. Bungee jumpers use safety gear when they jump. They use special cords called bungee cords. Bungee cords stretch easily. They allow jumpers to fall long distances without hitting the ground.

Men and women of many ages enjoy bungee jumping. Almost any adult in good physical condition can bungee jump. People weighing less than 75 pounds (34 kilograms) cannot bungee jump in most places. In the

Bungee jumpers use bungee cords to jump from high places.

United States, children under 18 can bungee jump only with their parents' permission.

Jump Sites

Bungee jumpers jump from places called jump sites. A jump site is a high and sturdy place that supports a bungee jumper's weight. Bridges, towers, and cranes are popular jump sites.

Some companies build jump sites. These companies build tall towers for bungee jumping. They charge people who bungee jump from their sites. Other companies sell jumps from hot air balloons.

Bridges were once the most common jump sites. But today, it is illegal to bungee jump from many bridges in the United States and Canada. In North America, there are only three legal jumping sites from bridges.

Some companies sell bungee jumps from towers.

Jump Masters

Jump masters are experienced bungee jumpers who help other jumpers. Jump masters know about bungee jumping safety and rules. They have special training. Even the most experienced bungee jumpers will not jump unless a jump master is nearby.

Jump masters perform many tasks. They help people find jump sites. They check the sites for safety. They check and handle all the jump gear. Often, two or more jump masters check gear for safety.

The Jump

Bungee jumpers start their jumps from jumping platforms. Jumping platforms look like small diving boards. They usually are 100 to 200 feet (30 to 61 meters) above the ground.

Bungee jumpers dive head-first off jump platforms. Jumpers may fall as fast as 60 miles (97 kilometers) per hour. Bungee cords

Jump masters help jumpers with their equipment.

stretch as jumpers near the end of their falls. The cords slow down the jumpers.

Bungee cords stop stretching and pull back when jumpers reach the end of their jumps. This is called a rebound or a "boing." Jumpers bounce back up during a rebound. Then, they fall again. Jumpers may rebound three or more times before they come to a stop.

Jump masters sometimes pull jumpers back up to the platform after a jump. Other times, they lower jumpers to the ground. Then the jump masters unhook the bungee jumpers from the bungee cords.

Bungee cords stretch to slow down jumpers' falls.

Chapter 2

History of Bungee Jumping

Bungee jumping came from Pentecost Island. Pentecost Island is in the South Pacific Ocean near Australia. The people of Pentecost Island call themselves the Bunlap tribe of Vanuatu. Bunlap men tie strong vines called lianas to their ankles. They then jump from towers. They call this land diving.

The Bunlap men land dive because of an old story. In the story, a Bunlap man chases his wife up a tall tree. The man and woman both

The idea for modern bungee jumping came from the people of Pentecost Island.

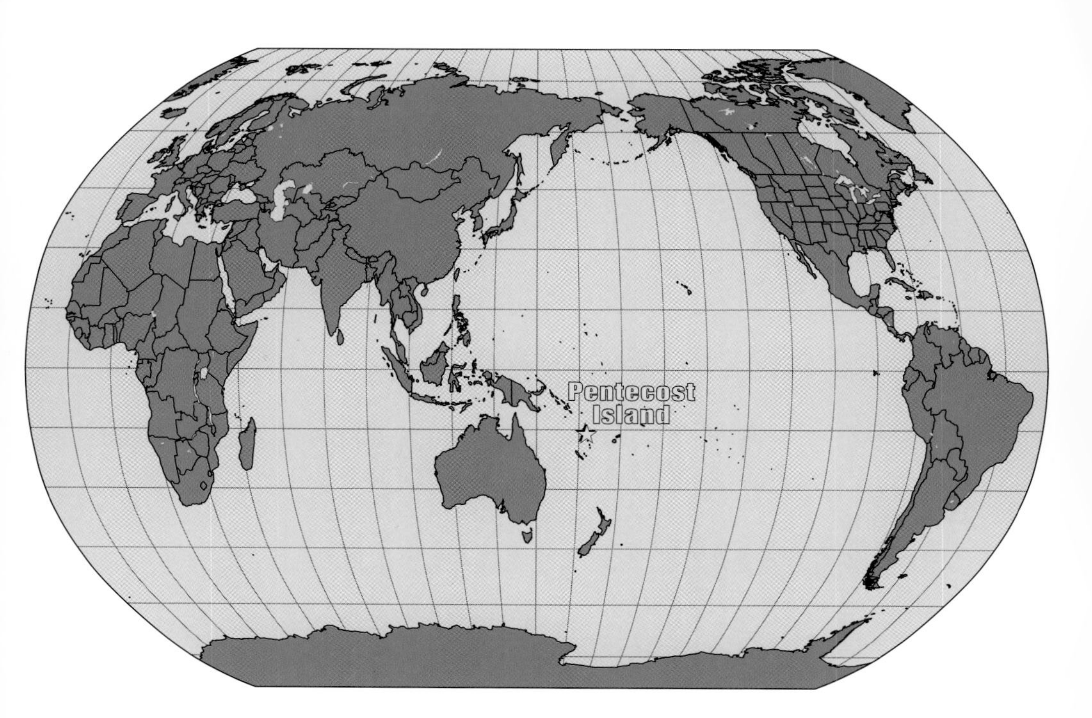

fall out of the tree. The man falls to the ground and dies. But the woman had tied a liana vine to her ankles. She swings safely from the end of the vine. The story says that Bunlap men learned about what the woman did. They practiced land diving so other women could not trick them.

Reports of Land Diving

U.S. soldiers visited Pentecost Island during World War II (1939–1945). They saw the

Bunlap men land diving. The soldiers told stories about these men when they returned to the United States.

Reporters from a magazine called *National Geographic* went to Pentecost Island in 1955. They wanted to learn about the Bunlap people. The reporters printed a story about the Bunlap in their magazine.

A British reporter named Kal Muller visited Pentecost Island in 1970. Muller asked the Bunlap to teach him to land dive. The Bunlap helped Muller jump from their tower. When he returned home, Muller wrote about his experiences for *National Geographic*.

Early Bungee Jumpers

Members of the Oxford Dangerous Sports Club of Great Britain read Muller's stories. The members wanted to land dive like the Bunlap. On April 1, 1979, several club members jumped off the Clifton Bridge in Bristol, England. They used bungee cords instead of vines.

Other people heard about the club members' bungee jumps. During the 1980s, people in North America and Europe began bungee jumping. In the 1990s, some state and federal governments passed laws against the sport. The government officials felt that it was too dangerous. But many bungee jumpers ignored the laws. They jumped in secret. Jumpers jumped early in the morning so they would not get caught.

Growth of Bungee Jumping

In 1987, a man named A. J. Hackett used a bungee cord to jump from a gondola in Europe. Gondolas are small compartments that carry people along wires above the ground. Hackett later used a bungee cord to jump from the Eiffel Tower in Paris, France. This jump helped the sport of bungee jumping become better known across the world.

Hackett wanted other people to try bungee jumping. He started to make his own bungee

Bungee jumping became popular during the late 1980s.

jumping equipment. In 1988, Hackett started one of the world's first commercial jump sites, in New Zealand. People had to pay to jump from Hackett's commercial site.

During the late 1980s, brothers John and Peter Kockelman started the first commercial jump sites in North America. They started a company called Bungee Adventures. The

company's first jump site was in Palo Alto, California. People paid $99 to bungee jump there.

By 1992, more than 1 million North Americans had tried bungee jumping. Many people had accidents. Some of these people suffered serious injuries. Some even died. The United States government became worried about the safety of the bungee jumpers. Many state governments passed laws to control bungee jumping.

Today, each state has its own laws about bungee jumping. Canada also has laws to control the sport. These laws follow a set of rules created by the North American Bungee Association (NABA). The set of rules is called the "Code of Safe Practice."

By 1992, more than 1 million North Americans had tried bungee jumping.

Chapter 3

Stunts and Competition

Most bungee jumpers jump for fun and excitement. Some jumpers also jump in competitions. Jumpers in competitions perform stunts such as flips and spins during their jumps.

Record Jumps

Some bungee jumpers try to set records for high jumps. In 1991, John Kockelman set a record by jumping 1,000 feet (305 meters) from a hot air balloon. In 1993, Chris Allum

Most bungee jumpers jump for fun and excitement.

set the record for the longest bungee jump from a bridge. Allum jumped 822 feet (251 meters) off a bridge at the New River Gorge in West Virginia.

Stunts

Some bungee jumpers do stunts while they jump. Experienced jumpers may do flips and spins as they fall. They may do stunts during their rebounds as well.

Stunt jumping is dangerous. Jumpers can become tangled in the bungee cords. Only experienced bungee jumpers should try stunts.

One popular stunt for experienced jumpers is to fall as close to the ground as possible. Jumpers figure exactly how long their bungee cords must be to make these jumps. They adjust the cords to stop their falls when they are only a few inches above the ground. This kind of jumping is very dangerous. Beginning bungee jumpers should never try this.

Some bungee jumpers touch the surface of a lake or pool during their jumps.

The X-Games

The first official bungee jumping competition was at the X-Games in 1995. The X-Games is a competition hosted each year by a television network called ESPN. People at the X-Games compete in many different extreme sports. The X-Games included bungee jumping competitions in 1995 and 1996. These were the first and only major bungee jumping competitions in the world.

At the X-Games, each jumper took three jumps off a 165-foot (50-meter) tower. Judges scored jumpers based on the stunts the jumpers performed. Judges added each jumper's two best scores for the final score. The top 15 jumpers advanced to a final round. The jumper with the highest score in this round won.

Bungee jumpers at the 1995 and 1996 X-Games performed stunts.

Chapter 4
Equipment

The equipment used for bungee jumping is very important. The gear must keep jumpers from falling too far. It also must protect jumpers while they fall. It must be strong enough not to break. Jumpers and jump masters must set up and store their equipment carefully. They must make sure none of it is damaged.

The Bungee Cord

The bungee cord is one of the most important pieces of equipment. Most bungee cords in North America actually are several cords tied

The bungee cord is one of the most important pieces of bungee jumping equipment.

Jump masters must make sure cords and harnesses are strong.

together. A cotton and nylon cover called a sheath holds the cords together. Sheaths protect the cords from dirt, air, and water. This keeps the cords strong.

Most bungee cords made in North America meet MIL-SPEC standards. MIL-SPEC stands for military specification. MIL-SPEC cords are strong enough to support heavy weights without breaking. MIL-SPEC cords also stretch consistently. This means a jumper can figure out exactly how far a cord will stretch during a jump. This length depends on a jumper's weight.

Each bungee cord has a set amount of rubber. The amount of rubber determines how far a certain weight will stretch the cord. Jump masters must know which cords are best for different jumpers. They base this on jumpers' weights. Jumpers can be injured if they do not use the right bungee cords.

Jump masters must make sure cords are strong. They must not use bungee cords too many times. Cords can wear out if they are used too often. Cords also can break if too much weight pulls on them.

The Harness

A harness connects a jumper to the bungee cord. This set of straps and buckles must be strong enough to support the jumper's weight.

The full-body harness is one of the safest and most common kinds of bungee jumping harnesses. A full-body harness wraps around the jumper's bottom and chest. A jump master fastens cords to these places on the jumper's body. Metal links called carabiners connect the bungee cord to the full-body harness.

Another kind of harness is the ankle harness. Ankle harnesses wrap around jumpers' lower legs and ankles. Jumpers often use backup harnesses with ankle harnesses. The backup harnesses help to keep the jumpers safe.

Jump Platforms

The jumper and the jump master stand on the jumping platform. Different jump sites have different jumping platforms. For example, hot air balloons may use small planks as jumping platforms.

The bungee cord is attached to an anchor point next to the jump platform. Anchor points are solid points that can support the weight of falling jumpers. Jump platforms and anchor points must be sturdy.

Ankle harnesses wrap around jumpers' lower legs and ankles.

Cooper

Other Equipment

Bungee jumpers wear a variety of safety equipment. Some wear helmets. Most jumpers wear gloves. Gloves protect jumpers' hands from rubbing against bungee cords. Some jumpers wear goggles to protect their eyes from wind and insects during a jump. Many jumpers wear pads under their harnesses. The pads keep the harnesses from rubbing against their skin.

Jump masters often place large air bags or pools of water below jump sites. Air bags and pools protect jumpers in case bungee cords stretch too far or break.

Some bungee jumpers wear helmets.

Tower
Jump Platform

Bungee Cord
Ankle Harness
Air Bag

Free Style

Chapter 5
Safety

Most bungee jumpers depend on their jump masters for safety. Jump masters have knowledge, professional training, and experience. They know when conditions are too dangerous for jumping. They can give jumpers tips on how to jump safely.

Safety Standards

Bungee jump sites must meet certain safety standards. These rules help keep jumpers safe. Standards vary from country to country. The North American Bungee Association (NABA)

Jump masters have knowledge, professional training, and experience.

STAFF

is one group that helps set standards in North America. The NABA's "Code of Safe Practice" includes the most common safety standards.

All bungee jumping equipment must meet safety standards set by the NABA. These standards cover items such as the materials used to make bungee cords and harnesses. They also tell manufacturers how strong equipment must be.

Jump Masters and Safety

Jump masters make sure bungee jumpers are safe. Jumpers must find jump masters they trust. Jumpers must do everything their jump masters tell them to do.

Most jump masters are experienced and well trained. They understand how all the bungee jumping equipment works. They have studied jump sites. They know how to keep jumpers safe.

Jump masters must maintain jumping equipment. They must check cords for damage between jumps. Most jump masters test

Jump masters tell jumpers about safety.

bungee cords after every 100 uses. They do this by testing how far the cords stretch under set conditions.

Jump masters often use static cords. These are backup cords that jumpers wear with regular bungee cords. Static cords protect jumpers if the regular bungee cords break.

Jump Site Safety

Jump sites must be safe and legal. Jumpers and jump masters inspect new jump sites carefully before jumping. They look for dangers such as unsteady jump platforms or obstacles. Obstacles can hurt jumpers who rebound into them. Obstacles include cables and power lines. Jumpers should avoid jump sites with obstacles nearby.

Jumpers and jump masters should check the wind at a jump site. Strong winds can cause jump sites to sway. Wind also can push jumpers into obstacles or cause them to go out of control.

Jump sites should be free of obstacles.

Hot Air Balloon Safety

Some bungee jumping companies sell jumps from hot air balloons. These companies must follow special rules. The Federal Aviation Administration (FAA) sets standards for flying aircraft. The FAA must give permission to companies that use hot air balloons for bungee jumping. Balloons used for bungee jumping must meet FAA standards. Licensed balloon pilots must fly the balloons.

Hot air balloons must support a jumper's weight without moving. Heavy jumpers may pull down small balloons. Many companies tie their balloons to the ground. This keeps the balloons steady. It also keeps the height of the balloons from changing. This allows jumpers to enjoy their sport safely.

A hot air balloon must support a jumper's weight without moving.

Words to Know

bungee cord (BUHN-jee KORD)—a rubber cord wrapped in cotton and nylon

carabiner (kair-uh-BEE-nur)—the metal link that connects a bungee cord to a full-body harness

commercial (kuh-MUR-shuhl)—operated to make a profit

gondola (GON-duh-luh)—a small compartment that carries people along a wire above the ground

harness (HAR-niss)—a set of straps and buckles that connects a bungee jumper to a bungee cord

jump master (JUHMP MASS-tur)—an experienced bungee jumper who assists other jumpers

MIL-SPEC (MIL-SPEK)—military specification; bungee cords made in the United States must meet MIL-SPEC standards.

sheath (SHEETH)—a cotton and nylon cover that holds a bungee cord together

To Learn More

Allen, Missy. *Dangerous Sports.* The Encyclopedia of Danger. New York: Chelsea House, 1993.

Italia, Bob. *Bungee Jumping.* Action Sports Library. Edina, Minn.: Abdo & Daughters, 1993.

Kidd, P. J. *Behind the Extreme Games.* Extreme Games. Edina, Minn.: Abdo & Daughters, 1999.

Useful Addresses

British Elastic Rope Sports Association (BERSA)
33A Canal Street
Oxford, Oxfordshire
OX 2 6BQ
England

Bungee Safety Consultant (North American Bungee Association)
P.O. Box 121
Fairview, OR 97024

Bungee Consultants International
22 Aldridge Way,
Nepean, ON K2G 4H8
Canada

Internet Sites

Bungee Safety Consultant (North American Bungee Association)
http://www.bungee.com

ESPN Sportszone
http://espn.sportszone.com/editors/xgames/bungee/

History of Bungee Jumping
http://espn.go.com/editors/xgames/bungee/history.html

Index